Kate Penney

June 1, 1995

Fun Is
A Feeling

*To all of our feelings
and the vision they bring.*

ILLUMINATION ARTS
PUBLISHING COMPANY, INC.
BELLEVUE, WASHINGTON

Fun Is
A Feeling

Words by Chara M. Curtis

Illustrations by Cynthia Aldrich

Concept by Chara and Cynthia

I once met a man who had so much fun
I just had to ask him how it was done.
He juggled my question a moment or two,
Then he laughed, "Fun or not…it's all up to you!

Fun isn't *something* or *somewhere* or *who*;
It's a feeling of joy that lives inside of you.
You can feel happy, or you can feel sad....
Joy comes from knowing no feeling is bad.

Treasure your feelings and treat them with care.
Pay close attention to the wisdom they share.
This is the way to become your best friend,
And then—you can have fun without end!

Fun can be found wherever you go,

But there's one more thing I think you should know.

Sometimes it hides, because fun LOVES to play,

And waits till you see things a different way.

Consider the courage of that little bug
Who jumped on your nose to give you a hug…
Or the soft, silken lace of a wondrous design
That a spider created as your valentine!

Feel the kiss of a raindrop, see the wink of a star—
Magic reminders of how loved you are.
Or picture yourself with a swashbuckling friend
Riding a whale to the Land of Pretend.

When you see things this way, you put joy in your heart.
And when your heart's full, you've done the first part.
The rest is so easy—what fun's all about—
Just open your heart…and LET YOUR FUN OUT!

Mermaids will spill from your bathwater spout
And glide to the sea on a rainbow of trout.
While sea lions slide from your slippery knees,
Porpoises balance on bubbles with ease.

cynthia aldrich '91

It's all what you make it. It's all what you see.
Only YOU can create how you want it to be!
The next time you're bored, make a smile from your frown…
Just stand on your head, and you've turned it around!

When you have chores and fun seems to run out,
Vacuum the hall with an elephant's snout!
Call on the elves to come lend a hand
And sweep up the stardust in your fairyland.

Not everyone's notion of fun is the same.
Some like it wild and some like it tame.
Some like the opera, some like the zoo,
And sometimes pretending is all you can do.

I'm so glad you've asked me about having fun—
A valuable question, when all's said and done—
For you make the world a more beautiful place
With the light in your eyes and the grin on your face.

cynthia aldrich '91

You're so important that each time you smile
The joy that you feel travels mile after mile.
It crosses the mountains and swims through the seas.
It flies through the air and tickles the trees!

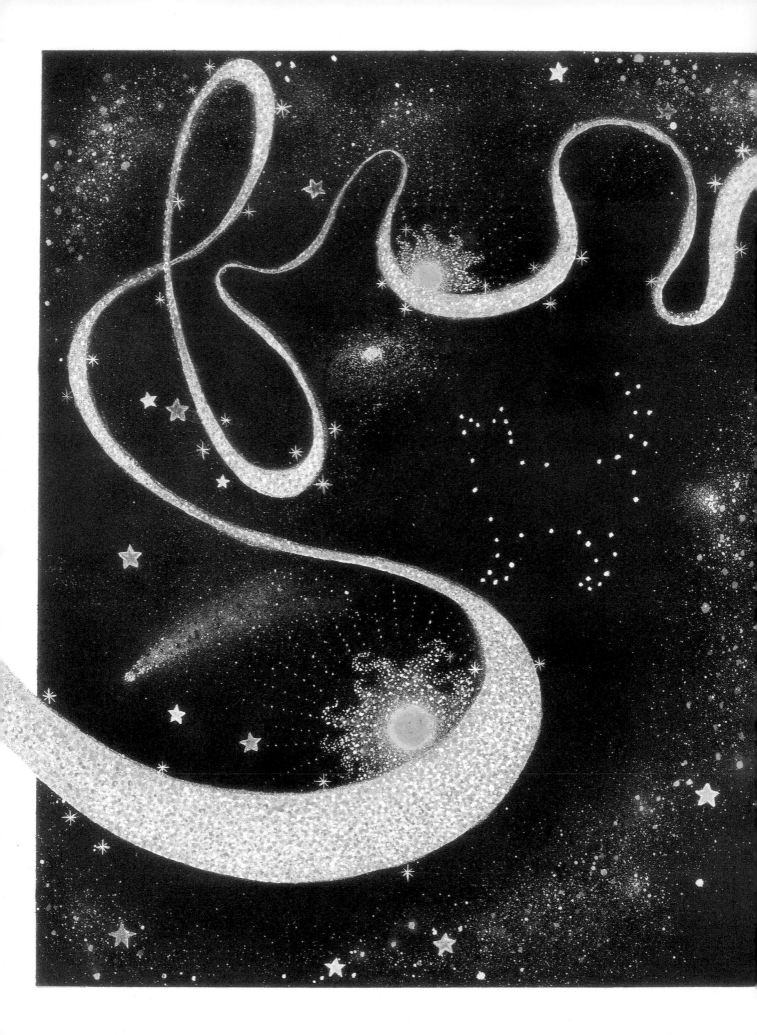

When you open your heart and your fun tumbles out,
News of it travels a heavenly route.
It soars through the galaxies, igniting each sun,
And the stars are ablaze…with your feeling of fun."

Chara M. Curtis seldom strays from her farm in the forests of Northwest Washington. Here she enjoys writing her rhymes—as well as living them. A bit intimidated by crowds, Chara generally prefers to shoo the mermaids from her tub before bathing. And having recently learned to avoid the sometimes devasting effects of elephant sneezes, she declares that she would not trade her life for anyone else's.

Cynthia Aldrich was born and raised in the Pacific Northwest. She graduated from the University of Washington in Seattle with a major in painting and graphic art. After studying at a private art school in California, she has pursued painting in various media as a way of creatively expressing her visions. The expression and exploration of feelings continues to be a central theme in Cynthia's work.

Her artworks, in a wide variety of media, are displayed in numerous private collections. Cynthia currently lives and works on Whidbey Island, Washington.

Look for *All I See Is Part of Me*
also from Illumination Arts
by Chara M. Curtis and Cynthia Aldrich.

Published in The United States of America
Printed by Toppan Printing Company of Singapore

Library of Congress Cataloging in Publication Data

Curtis, Chara M. 1950–
          Fun is a feeling / words by Chara M. Curtis ; illustrations by
Cynthia Aldrich ; concept by Chara and Cynthia.
              p. cm.
          Summary: A child discovers that the joy of life comes from
within and that attitude is all-important.
          ISBN 0-935699-04-X : $14.95
          1. Children's poetry, American. [1. American poetry.]
I. Aldrich, Cynthia, 1947–   . II. Title.
PS3553.U694F8   1992
811'.54—dc20

Library of Congress Number 91-41875

I L L U M I N A T I O N   A R T S
PUBLISHING COMPANY, INC.
P.O. BOX 1865
BELLEVUE, WA 98009